Virtual Reality 101:
All the stuff you need to know
(plus a little more.)

Dedicated to the amazing woman who is my rock, my strength, and my travel companion across the world, my wife Anu . And also to my son Michael, who's curiosity into all things tech led to his career in VR, and inspired me to do the research that ending up being this book, so I could keep up with him.

FORWARD
Virtual Reality 101: Everything you need to know (plus a little more)

We are gradually getting to a point in technological advancement where the "crazy" and 'Wow! That's so cool!" things we read about in sci-fi novels and see in our movies may no longer be "someday" fiction, but may quickly become everyday interactions in our lives. The line between today's fantasy and tomorrows reality is a constantly moving one. The growth of our technology is exponentially pushing the frontier in our real, and virtual, world past preconceived limits.

Would you like to experience the thrill of swimming with dolphins deep in the ocean without the fear of being in danger from sharks? What about being in a movie theater, playing a video game, watching your favorite team, interacting and cheering with your friends, while still being physical present in your own home? These and many more types of experiences are quickly becoming likely in the near future as the use of virtual reality technology continue to expand.

In this book we will look at what virtual reality is, how it started, and how we use it today. We will also look at some of the fields it is disrupting, creating and destroying. We will discuss the differences between virtual reality and augmented reality and we will look at the economic drivers behind their development.

Finally, we will touch upon the moral and ethical considerations that a fully immersive technology has a a culture.

We will even engage on a fanciful "how far can this go" conversation in the end chapters.

I hope you enjoy reading this and it helps answer your questions about virtual reality.

-Terry M. Taylor

Chapter 1   What is virtual reality?

Chapter 2   Virtual reality: From the past to the present

Chapter 3   How is virtual reality created?

Chapter 4   How does virtual reality work?

Chapter 5   Types of virtual reality

Chapter 6   Current areas of use of 3D Virtual Reality

Chapter 7   Augmented Reality vs Virtual Reality

Chapter 8   When Virtual Reality meets Artificial Intelligence

Chapter 9   Virtual Reality and The Changing World of Business

Chapter 10   Emerging trends for future Virtual Reality

Chapter 11   Anticipated impacts of emerging Virtual Reality

Chapter 12   Challenges and concerns

Chapter 13 Limitations that need to be addressed for VR adoption

Chapter 14   Towards realism: Creating better Virtual Reality technology with higher immersion and spatial presence

Chapter 15   Virtual Reality: The Caution

Chapter 16   Can 'Virtual Reality' ever become 'Actual Reality'?

Chapter 17   Content is King
Chapter 18   Conclusion

CHAPTER 1
WHAT IS VIRTUAL REALITY

Virtual reality is the term used to describe computer-generated three-dimensional images, simulating a desired real-world environment. This environment can be interacted with and explored by the user. Currently, the experience of virtual reality is still largely limited to sight and sound. Haptic feedback (touch), and the feedbacks of taste and smell are gradually being explored as the boundaries of technologies are expanding to make the experiences more realistic.

As humans, the world we know today and the environment we are conscious of, is the result of the stimuli and responses perceived by our five senses; sight, hearing, touch, taste and smell.

The concept of "virtual reality" stems from the idea that if we can present a different set of information perceptible to the human sense organs, the sensory information generate can make the brain believe that it is in another 'real' world. Thus, a controlled or invented version of reality can be presented to the brain as "real".

In current technology, this means head-mounted devices, gloves and omni-direction treadmills that are used to generate a simulation of the real world. This allows the user to engage in experiences that transcend time and geographical borders. Its revolutionary impacts range from real estate, shopping, social and telepresence, tourism and exploration, psychology and meditation, gaming, education and simulation, artistry, design and entertainment.

CHAPTER 2
FROM THE PAST TO THE PRESENT

Our concept of Virtual Reality has evolved over time. As science fiction writers tap into popular culture expressing its desires and creating compelling fiction, scientists are inspired and businesses flock to provide a solution for those desires. Currently when discussing virtual reality, the conversation focuses on the delivery method, usually the headset. But the concept of virtual reality predates when head-mounted displays were first made. What used to be seen only in sci-fi films is now fast becoming reality. It is very difficult to state the exact date when the concept of virtual reality started, but most researchers, experts, and writers will agree that it was approximately the 1950s when it started gaining some popular attention and recognition.

The Past

In 1938, Antonin Artaud described the illusory nature of characters and objects in the theater "la réalité virtuelle" in a collection of essays, "Le Theatre et son double". The English translation of this book, published in 1958 as "The Theater and its Double", is the earliest published use of the term "virtual reality". The first "mainstream" use of the term "virtual reality" was used in *The Judas Mandala*, a 1982 science fiction novel by Damien Broderick. [1]
Although some experts will say the history of virtual reality can be traced back to the 1800s, when photography started, most will point to the earliest example of a practical and active use of "virtual reality" can be traced to Morton Heilig. Morton was one the founding fathers of cinematography in the mid twentieth century. In 1958, Heilig designed a single user console called Sensorama to create a fascinating movie experience. See picture belowof Morton and his Sensorama.

---

[1] https://en.wikipedia.org/wiki/Virtual_reality

2

Morton acquired enough backing to manufacture a single unit in 1962. It was featured a stereoscopic display, speakers, fans and a moving chair. With these components the Sensorama was able to display stereoscopic 3-D images in a wide-angle view, provide body tilting, supply stereo sound, and also had components for wind and aromas to be triggered during the film.

The Sensorama was one of the earliest examples of what is now known as "multimodal technology"[3]. It possessed a certain degree of immersion as it simulates audio-visual experiences for the user. Helig saw cinematography and theater as opportunity for an activity that would engage all human senses (especially sight and sound) to give users a sense of presence. Although it was critically well accepted, it was a not widely adopted due to lack of financial backing. The static and bulky nature of the unit also provided barriers to its widespread acceptance. Despite it being a financial disappointment, this invention marked a vital stage in development and acceptance of virtual reality.

---

[2] https://www.techradar.com/news/wearables/forgotten-genius-the-man-who-made-a-working-vr-machine-in-1957-1318253/2

[3] **Multimodal technologies** refer to all **technologies** combining features extracted from different modalities (text, audio, image, etc.). This covers a wide range of component **technologies**: Audiovisual Speech Recognition. Audiovisual Person Identification

Further research on Heilig's Sensorama lead the Philco Corporation to create the world's first head-mounted display (HMD) in the early 1960's.

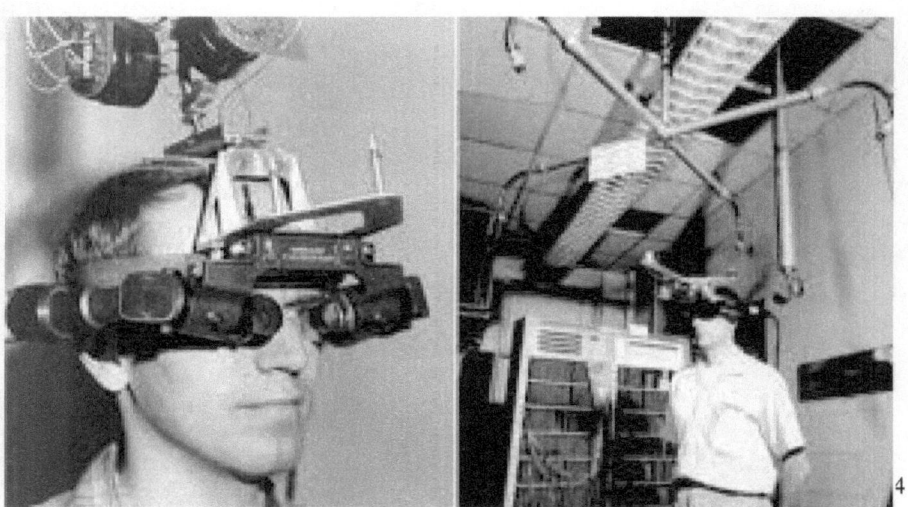

They made it more acceptable by incorporating a head tracking device in the HMD, which made it capable for the device the simulate the view of the user by using the head tracker. The military saw uses for this breakthrough and adopted it, giving the device wider acceptance. A major breakthrough was made by Ivan Sutherland in 1965. He incorporated the HMD together with a computer, creating what he called an "Ultimate Display". The images created were more real and the interface possessed better interactive features for the user. Although the device had to be suspended in the air during usage because of its bulkiness and weight, the tracking property still made it more successful than earlier inventions and a leap forward in delivering a more realistic experience.

The first time that usable technology was referred to as a "Virtual Reality" was in 1987, when Michael McGreevy of NASA created the first "virtual environment workstation". This offered a wider field of field and was comparatively more affordable.

---

[4] https://www.wareable.com/wearable-tech/origins-of-virtual-reality-2535

From this point, the focus shifted from military to commercial to the games industry of the early 1990s, as gamers adopted the technology.

Virtuality Group was one of the first to adopt it, followed by Sega who, through the advancement of the virtual reality technology in the mid-1980s, released the games Hang-On and After Burner as some of the first arcade games that make use of hydraulic cabinet functionality and force feedback control. In 1988 Sega also released the 360-degree rotating machine R-360. "The R-360 was an arcade cabinet produced by Sega. It had two axes of movement, allowing the player to rotate freely as the cabinet mimics the in-game action, including turning the cabinet completely upside down. Sega used the acronym SDMS (Servo Drive Movement System) for the cabinet's system.

5

---

[5] https://segaretro.org/R360

The R-360 was also known for its many interior safety features such as a safety harness similar to a roller coaster harness, two seatbelts which attached to the harness, and an Emergency Stop Button. Its exterior safety features included an Emergency Stop button on the attendant tower, a series of pressure-sensitive mat intrusion systems which would trigger an alarm when any of the mats were stepped on while the game was in motion, and due to how large and heavy the main cabinet was, a plexiglass fence surrounded the cabinet to avoid anyone from getting too close to the cabinet."[6] High costs and competitive pressures forced Sega to reorganize away from hardware and their position as an innovator in this field.

Over the years, virtual reality machines have been downsized and the cost continue to decrease. This has allowed for a further penetration into many fields of business as new and innovative ways of taking advantage of the technology are being discovered with each change in costs and scalability.

From the Present, looking to the Future
Currently, no virtual reality hardware or software has been able to give a full immersion experience, but the industry now cuts across many fields. Beside the games industry, many fields including a wide variety in business, entertainment and education are some of the most impacted. Even though the "Holy Grail" of full immersion has yet been achieved, the current virtual reality experience now gives a greater user presence and an overwhelming experience than it could even a few short years ago.
Technological innovations driven by smartphone and gaming industries are at the forefront the virtual reality technology explosion. Companies like Google can push mainstream adoption when they produce items like "Google Cardboard", where users can simply slide in their phones to have a basic type of virtual reality experience.

---

[6] https://en.wikipedia.org/wiki/R-360

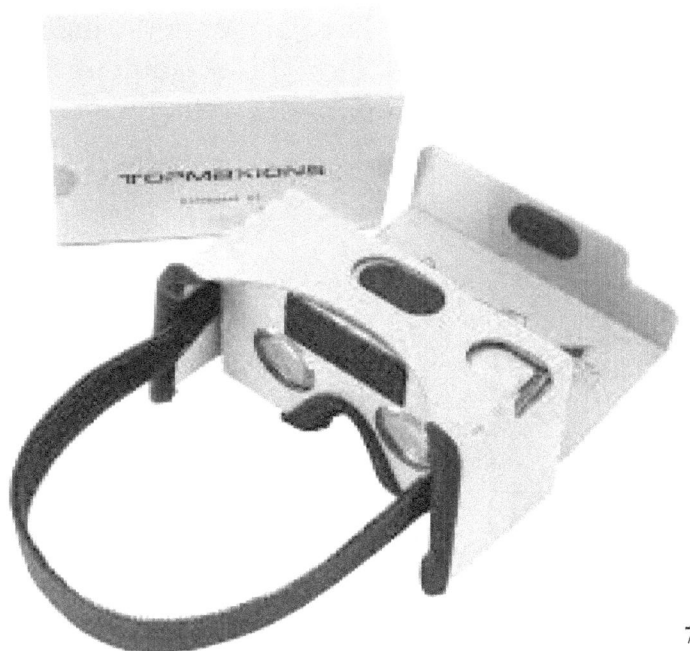

7

Samsung followed suit by launching and mass production of the "Galaxy Gear" with the added feature of gesture control.

8

---

[7] https://www.amazon.com/Cardboard-Topmaxions-Virtual-Reality-Compatible/dp/B01C2PA0KK

[8] https://www.amazon.com/Cardboard-Topmaxions-Virtual-Reality-Compatible/dp/B01C2PA0KK

In 2014 Facebook bought in and become a huge player in the industry by investing $2 billion to purchase Oculus Rift. This is a bold move told virtual reality forecasters that the future for the technology seems very bright.

9

Presently the major players in the industry are: Facebook's Oculus Rift and HTC Vive. Continued development by Microsoft with their Xbox One, and now Xbox X (Project Scorpio), together with Sony's Daydream will increasing penetration into the market but are yet to be fully developed, released and accepted by mainstream. More phone makers are also developing the virtual reality market. Sales of these units continue to climb as the following quote shows:
"According to a report from Canalys, in Q3 of 2017, Sony shipped 490,000 PlayStation VR headsets, Oculus shipped 210,000 Rift headsets and HTC shipped 160,000 Vive units."[10]

---

[9] https://www.caseking.de/en/oculus-rift-virtual-reality-headset-touch-motion-controller-gavr-033.html

[10] https://techcrunch.com/2017/11/28/virtual-reality-headset-unit-sales-are-slowly-improving/

Below, we will take a look at each of the biggest players in the virtual reality industry, reviewing their current status, and commenting on their prospects for the future.

Oculus Rift: this device was initially owned by an independent company but later purchased by Facebook in March 2017. But prior to Facebook's purchase, earlier versions of the Rift were made. It is now owned and run by Oculus virtual reality, a division of Facebook Inc.
At its inception, founder Palmer Luckey launched a Kickstarter campaign in 2012. It raised $2.5 million and was enough to produce a protype and then several styles of prototypes after. The Rift has gone through various pre-production models since the Kickstarter campaign, around five of which were demonstrated to the public. Two of these models were shipped to backers, labelled as 'development kits'; the DK1 in mid 2013, and DK2 in mid 2014, to give developers a chance to develop content on time for the Rift's release. Because of the excitement generated by the positive reception of the release, both were also purchased by a large number of enthusiasts who wished to get an early preview of the technology.
The Rift DK1 launched into the market on March 29, 2013 and had many improvements over the original prototype. It had a 7-inch screen and a lower switching time reducing latency and motion blur. The screen door effect in earlier version was also reduced. In addition to the device had a wider field of view [more than 110-degree vertical and 90-degrees horizontal]. This was also unprecedented in earlier versions. Other added qualities include a resolution of 1280x800 and replaceable lenses that can achieve dioptric correction.
The DK1 was followed by the introduction of the HD prototype later in 2013. In this, the poor resolution of the DK1 was corrected. Later the following versions were further released to further increase user presence and immersion. The prototypes include crystal cove, Development Kit 2 and the Crescent Bay prototypes. These were developed between January and September, 2014.

The Rift has a Pentile OLED display, 1080×1200 resolution per eye, a 90 Hz refresh rate, and 110° field of view. It has integrated headphones which provide a 3D audio effect, rotational and positional tracking. The positional tracking system, called "Constellation", is performed by a USB stationary infrared sensor that is picking up light that is emitted by IR LEDs that are integrated into the head-mounted display. The sensor normally sits on the user's desk. This creates 3D space, allowing for the user to use the Rift while sitting, standing, or walking around the same room.[11]

In 2016 Oculus released the consumer version of the Rift, sold at $599.99. This consumer version improved on the crescent bay prototype by having features such as 360-degree position tracking, more than 90 Hz per-eye display, and a resolution higher than the DK2.

The Oculus Rift hardware comes two OLED panels with 1080x1200 resolution and a persistence rate (how long they an display an image as measured in "per milliseconds of each frame") of 2. This gives it a higher quality global refresh, high refresh rate and low persistence, creating a higher presence and immersion experience for the user.

Requirements for use-
The minimum system for oculus rift is intel core i3 or AMD FX 4350, a graphics card of GeForce GT960, two USB 3.0 port and a single USB 2.0 port, all on a Windows 8 Operating system.
The Rift also has a positional tracking system called the constellation sensor. It monitors the position of the head and body parts of the system. It is used to give a "room scale" virtual reality. In addition to the position tracker is motion controller. This is a set of handheld devices that comes with the new versions of Rift. It is worn on both hands simulating the user's hand movements in the virtual environment. There are also buttons on it that can be used in games that involve firing.

---

[11] https://en.wikipedia.org/wiki/Oculus_Rift

In order to meet up with future demands and demands in technology, Oculus Virtual Reality has revealed its plan that it will be releasing new versions of the Rift every two or three years.

Most recently in 2018, Oculus launch a wire free version called the Oculus Go. This is from there website- "Easily enter virtual reality with no PC or wires attached. Oculus Go is a Standalone VR headset made to fit you. Designed with breathable fabrics, adjustable straps and our best lenses yet."[12]

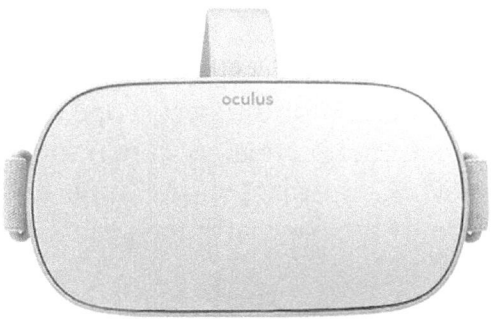

HTC Vive: This was launched in 2015 during HTC's World Congress. With the room scale tracking technology, together with its room scale tracking controllers, the user can move in a 3D space and interact with the simulated environment with better accuracy.

---

[12] https://www.oculus.com/go/

[13]

Just like the Oculus Rift, the Vive has a refresh rate of 90 Hz and a resolution of 1080x1200. One of its unique advantages is that it uses a total of 70 infrared sensors. The combination of the gyroscope, accelerometer and MEMS (micro electromagnetical systems) to track the motion of the user. The sensors works best in a room that is about 15ft x 15ft, and can track the position of the user with the precision to within fractions of a millimeter.

Another interesting feature of the Vive being used as part of the 'Chaperon' safety system is that it can identify the motion of any object in the room through its front-facing camera. This helps in notifying the user to steer clear of obstacles.

The current HTC Vive devices support not only the Microsoft Windows operating system, but also Linux is also supported as of February 2017, and integration with the MacOS was commenced in June 2017. In addition, Oculus Rift games can now be played on the HTC Vive.

Although HTC rapidly innovating both its hardware and software platforms, the future may not be too rosy for the Vive. Facebook is already working on slashing prices for the Rift. LG is also entering the market with a sleek design. Analysts feel that the Vive must find ways to innovate to remain competitive.

---

[13] https://www.google.com/search?q=htc+vive&client=firefox-b-ab&source=lnms&tbm=isch&sa=X&ved=0ahUKEwjO4JTgkvjdAhWJAnwKHYH0DSEQ_AUIDygC&biw=1680&bih=886&dpr=2#imgrc=9iaJ9d7TKoCKgM:

Samsung Gear VR by Samsung Electronics was released on late 2015 at a cost of $99.99.

As of this writing, more than 5 million devices have been sold. It has the advantage in its affordability and a large app library, and the software synchronizes well with Samsung phones. The Samsung S8 and S9 fits well into the new Gear virtual reality strategy. Because of its ease of use and compatibility with its phone line, the Samsung Gear VR is hailed for being a great entry level experience for virtual reality users.

The Samsung device is pioneering the use of mobile phones as the display of a headset. Although the technology of mobile phones was not as advanced as we have now, Samsung invested with the research internally. They further increased the research on using a VR headset with smartphones with the success of the launch of the Galaxy S4 in 2013.

The first fully compatible phone with the Gear virtual reality was the Galaxy Note 4. Since then there have been many prototypes of the Gear VR, among these, in the order of their release:

The SM-R320 (which was the first release)

SM-R321 (which supported Galaxy S6 and S6 Edge and added a USB port)

SM-R322 (which was lighter and supported six Samsung Galaxy Devices).

---

[14] https://www.samsung.com/global/galaxy/gear-vr/

Other versions include SM-R323 (which enabled data transfer, with increased field of view and a flat track pad), and now the SM-R324, released on 29 March 2017, supporting the Galaxy S8 smartphone. When used with Samsung Galaxy phones, the Gear VR acts as the controller with its field of view and inertial measurement unit for rotational tracking. In this case, the phone now acts as the display. The Gear VR is designed to support a Notion to Photon Latency less than 20 milliseconds with a field of view of about 101 degrees for the R323. Oculus Rift is the main software distributor for the Gear VR.
Google Daydream View: owned by Google and officially released on October 4, 2016

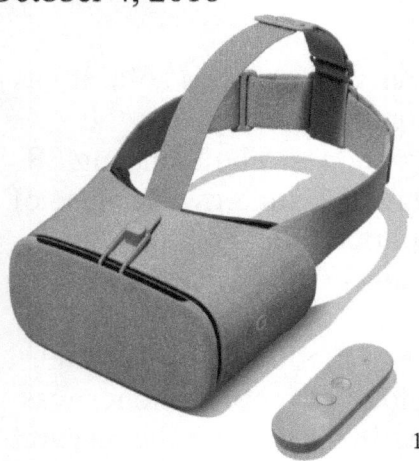
15

The Daydream View uses the android platform as its operating system. It cost about $79 on the average and is hailed as the lightest of all current headsets. The headset is made compatible for Daydream-adapted phones. The phone can be used as the display of the headset through the lenses.
The headset is lightweight when compared with others and has a better virtual reality viewing through its use of the capacitive nubs and NFC chips. Users also say that the headset rests more weight on the forehead than the cheeks, which helps in relieving possible neck stress for some users.

---

[15] https://developers.google.com/vr/discover/daydream-view

The device also comes with rechargeable wireless controllers and on-board sensors that are used to relate with the virtual world and tracks the motion and the orientation of the user's hands.

Since the Daydream View is more of a "mobile virtual reality platform" built to be compatible with mobile phones, Google has given authorized eight different Android manufacturers to come up with hardware that will make the phone compatible with virtual reality device. The companies are Alcatel, Asus, ZTE, Huawei, LG, HTC and Samsung.

CHAPTER 3
HOW IS A VIRTUAL REALITY CREATED?

What does it take to create a virtual reality experience?

In general, virtual reality devices are made up of a screen, worn on the face, a head piece. The head piece (usually called a head-mounted device) strapped to the user's head brings a small rendered image to each eye, and the users brain combines the image forming a 3-dimensional simulation.

The lens directly in front of the eyes in the head mounted device (HMD) is not where these images are coming directly from. The lenses merely possess magnifying capabilities, so the projected image can fill the user's field of view. They are placed between each eye and the images generated on a screen. That is we call them goggles (plural). To create adequate visual realism, the visual screens operates at a minimum frame rate of 60 frames per second. This, together with a wide field of view are the minimum requirement needed to avoid motion sickness and "stuttering".

Inside the HMD is a combination of motion tracking devices such accelerometer, magnetometer and gyroscope, which is a motion-simulating device. This moves in relation to how a user moves his head and consequently sends a sense of motion to the brain. The gyroscope moves as your head moves in the x, y and z axes within what is referred to as 6DoF [six degrees of freedom]. This head tracking is most effective when it has a minimum latency of 50 milliseconds or less. The lower the latency, the more realistic the motion is.

In addition to this, some HMDs have sensors that can track the body motion of the user, so that he can see the effect when he bends down or jumps up, walks or even runs. Devices with good refresh rate will create images with low latency, which helps the motion experience in the virtual environment to be at a realistic rate as if the user would see in the physical world. Some devices also come with gloves that simulates hand and finger movement while giving a haptic feedback to the user.

Also, some devices incorporate headphones for audio simulations. There are apps preinstalled in the device that enables sound to either fade or increase as the user moves further away or towards the source of sound.

Research is also on going on eye tracking in HMDs. With this you do not need to turn your head before your view of the virtual environment changes. According the experts, this will be achieved by using infrared sensor monitors inside the HMD. This will increase realism in the view of depth of field, and thus giving a higher immersion. This is simply because what obtains now in virtual reality is a visual effect where every object, irrespective of the distance from the user is at the same degree of sharpness.

As the technology gets more advanced and compelling, the senses of smell and taste are gradually being added.

CHAPTER 4
HOW DOES VIRTUAL REALITY WORK?

Basically, the concept of virtual reality is the simulation of the real world through multi-faceted 3D dimensional images. The more real it can be, the more engaging it will be for the user. The extent of realness of virtual reality depends on the three features: interaction, imagination and immersion.

- Interaction: Interaction in virtual reality can be experienced in six different ways. Ranging from the simplest to the more advanced. These are: no-interaction, gaze interaction, device-assisted interaction, unassisted interaction, feedback and speed of thought.

- No interaction: this is the earliest, simplest and the most basic interaction modes. In this you can only see the images as programmed into the device. It's more like watching a movie from a fixed stand-point. You have no interaction or control over the artificial environment.
- Gaze interaction: this is a bit more experiential than the first stage above. You can mere focus or gaze at a particular object or element in the simulated environment in order to have greater clarity. This places restriction on the free movement and has been described as being too slow for realism
- Assisted interaction: most virtual reality technologies are currently at this stage. this is also called device interaction. When you hold something in one or both hands this is usually achieved when holding something in either one or both to simulate your hand movement in the unreal world creating greater interaction. Example is the wizard wands of the PlayStation virtual reality.

- Unassisted interaction: this is one of the start points future virtual reality seems to be focusing on. This enables you to track all your body movements without wearing or holding any assisted device. The downside to this interaction is you cannot seem to get a feedback to where you really are as it relates to touch. In example, even though you can move your hand to touch an object, you won't get any feedback (besides visual) that you already have the object touched.
- Feedback: this technology is still being researched by the virtual reality industry. The interaction is termed 'feedback' when you can feel the impulses and stimuli of the simulated environment. Imagine actually feeling the gravity when climbing up a stair of you can feel the breeze of the unreal environment blowing against your skin. In these scenarios, you don't struggle to experience the environment. It interacts with not only all the five senses but also with your nervous system. The reality is not just seen or heard, but can also be felt.
- Speed of Thought: this is the destination most virtual reality technologies are aiming at. This technology can enable you to create an environment and be in it in the virtual world simply by thing about it. With the brain computer interface technology being more advanced by the day, virtual reality interaction at the speed of though may not be too difficult a dream to achieve.
- Immersion: This is the perception or state of consciousness of being physically present and involved in a simulated environment. It is the perception of being present in a digitally-simulated environment. Through the interaction of a network of 3D images, sound and other stimuli, you feel a sense of realism or what some term as the suspension of unbelieve. This means that the degree to which the simulated environment mimics reality through sights, sounds and other stimuli, determines whether you will experience a partial or complete suspension of unbelieve.

When immersion is at its peak, you will be able to interact with the digital environment in a natural and intuitive way. Experts have opined that realizing full virtual reality immersion may not occur until the year 2040. This will be a period where virtual reality can be experience by all the five senses of humans: sight, sound, touch, smell and taste. Asides from visual and auditory feedbacks that current technology possesses, there will be a need for olfactory feedback (smell replication), gustation feedback (taste replication) and tactile feedback (force and haptics feedbacks).

- Spatial presence: This is beyond immersion and it is characteristic unique only to virtual reality. Until spatial presence makes you feel you have been teleported into another real environment, realism cannot be said to have been fully achieved. Virtual presence is when fully experience can be magical. The sensation is indescribable. As the virtual reality technology gets more popular and accepted, one key factor that will decide who leads the market is the ability to create that stimulating experience from simulated but yet realistic computer-generated experience. Future virtual reality is currently looking to technologies that can help improve spatial presence of the users. The major factors being worked on include the following: lower latency, wider field of view, adequate resolution, adequate refresh rate, low pixel resistance, rock solid tracking, optics and optical calibration.

CHAPTER 5
TYPES OF VIRTUAL REALITY

The original intention of virtual reality is for the users to experience full immersion. Where they will no longer feel they are interacting with a device but feel present in the simulated world, where the virtual world is fully perceived as totally real. But based on the needs of various fields and the level of technological advancements, less immersive types of virtual reality are being used.

- Non-immersive: This, as the name suggests, is a passive form of virtual reality. Some of the senses like sight and sound are simulated but the user has no sense of being physically present in the environment. This is more like using a desktop computer, where the user views the virtual environment via monitor of even a head mounted display but can only interact with it through the mouse, keyboard or touchpad. Despite these, much of the technology used by non-immersive virtual reality is the same with that used in fully-immersive virtual reality. The difference is in the advancement.
- The advantage of this is that they do not require the best resolution and hence it is less costly. No sense of immersion is observed, and the user is still very much aware of his physical environment. Another benefit of this type of virtual reality is that it offers evolutionary compatibility. This means that it is easier for users to adapt to its use because the main means of interacting with the simulated world still remains the mouse and keyboard.
- In addition to the aforementioned benefits, non-immersive virtual reality creates lower challenges in hardware. The hardware configuration that will adequately run a non-immersive virtual reality software may be grossly inadequate to run a fully immersive software.
- One of the disadvantages of this is the lack of the sense of perceivable scale due to its non-immersiveness.

- Apart from is use in the gaming worlds, non-immersive virtual reality is used in enhancing motor performances for heart and stroke rehabilitation.

Semi-immersive virtual reality: this makes use of devices that can produce some immersive characteristics while the user is still aware of his immediate physical environment. An instance of semi-immersive virtual reality is used in flight simulators where the user is placed in front of a large, concave screen with very high resolution similar to what one experience sitting close to a cinema screen. The user will remain aware of his physical environment consisting of the cockpit and chair. There is no use of a head-mounted display or a data glove.

Fully immersive virtual reality: This is the virtual reality that can be said to be achieved when there is full awareness that the simulated environment is real. It the presentation of an artificial environment, digitally simulated with an attendant belief by the user that the perception derived from its usage is real.

The more an artificial environment is made to correctly simulate a real scenario, the more immersive it is judged to be. At this stage, disbelieve is fully suspended and the user fully engages in the environment.

There are some characteristics of virtual reality that increases the immersiveness of a virtual reality environment. These include the physical interaction of the user with the virtual objects in the scene, ability of the user to move freely within the confines of the virtual environment, a realistic sense of scale, conformance to the human vision and continuity of the surroundings.

Other qualities that determine immersiveness are the ability to give a haptic feedback, smell and taste feedbacks and correct sound-to-position simulations.

Presently, the global virtual reality market is worth more than USD 4.29 Billion. The market is much more competitive, with investors churning out newer and more immersive games and device, captivating the younger generation in unprecedented ways. Gradually the contents of gaming consoles have taken over the gaming world from PCs and mobile phones.

See the below chart to show the projected adoptive curve of virtual reality devices.[16]

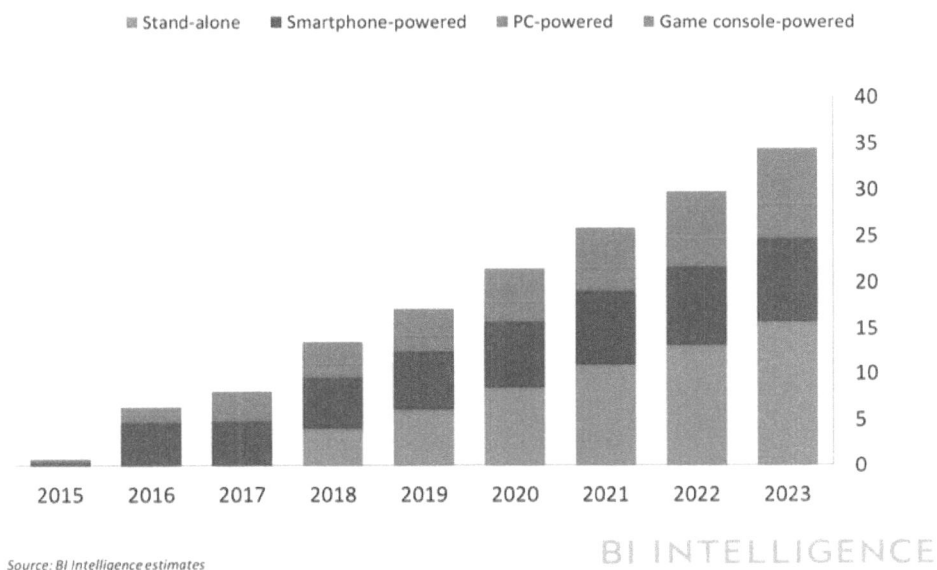

An example of a fully immersive environment is the CAVE. CAVE is the terminology used in describing the virtual environment where the user experiences full immersion. It stands for Cave Automatic Virtual Environment. This experience is achieved by directing projectors to the walls of cube-shaped room.

The user is placed inside the cube with 3D glasses on to enable him view graphics generated by the cube. These 3D glasses have sensors that tracks the user's movement, while the computers, through the projectors controls the audio and visuals giving the user an immersive motion capture.

Generally speaking, the more immersive a virtual reality gets, the closer we are to a paradigm shift in how we interact with the world. Experiences and possibilities will be unprecedented.

---

[16] https://www.businessinsider.com/the-vr-hardware-report-2018-3

Examples of this type of technology are already being adopted into main stream environments such as malls and gaming rooms.

- Collaborative virtual reality [CVE]: a virtual environment is said to be collaborative if it supports the participation and interrelationship between many participants in the virtual world in real time over large distances. This means that the simulated environment is shared.

It is a multi-person networked virtual reality environment connecting users from different locations around the globe into one simulated environment. The ways be work, play, interact and communicate will change drastically from the usual norm.

Virtual reality creates a dynamic way to work, communicate and interact, where people in different locations can share information in real time. It is made more effective by engaging data consistency models such as data ownership, Centralized primary model and distributed primary model. The technology is increasingly being used in work environments. In business, it is believed that CVR will help in providing a flexible and global workforce, serve as an essential training tool, reduce production and overhead costs and increase profit.

"A recent survey by Dell Inc., Intel Corp. and consultants Penn Schoen Berland, found that 57% of employees around the world prefer face-to-face conversations with colleagues. Again, this is where VR has potential to excel and disrupt the current way meetings occur.

Imagine working environments where you virtually see someone standing in front of you. You can see them, the working space, their non-verbal cues. It's as if you're working there together. Just think of the applications for teams managing projects across the globe? Now consider, too, how it might change our workspace and collaboration use cases.

We saw how messaging apps and other tools have evolved business communications, what about virtual workspaces? The potential is vastly unexplored."

Examples of the other fields where collaborative virtual reality is used are the architecture and construction, medicine and healthcare, courtrooms, marketing, military and medical training, entertainment, education and arts. Already in the business market it could change the way people collaborate, present information and host conference calls. Although a new technology can open a vast amount of possibilities to improve the workplace, we still have a long way to go to understand the full potential of VR.

CHAPTER 6
CURRENT AREAS OF USE OF VIRTUAL REALITY

Gaming: the history of virtual reality won't be complete without mentioning virtual reality games. The games were made to provide users with alternative reality. The creation of the Nintendo games in the early 1990's was the beginning of virtual reality hardware. The success rate was low in succeeding years due to unaffordability. Other game consoles have like the PlayStation are now prevalent despite its high cost due to higher immersive capacities, offering more interactive entertainment. Advertisement and marketing: in advertising, 360 virtual reality is fast becoming the new reality. The immersion and interactive qualities it displays an unequalled vantage point over all other advertising and marketing options. Business owners are fast considering it as the acquisition becomes more affordable each year. Even politicians are adopting the technology to reach voters. In 2008, the candidate Barrack Obama's campaign "bought ads" in video games. Ads for the candidate appeared in a total of 18 video games, including the extremely popular "Guitar Hero" and "Madden 09". "These ads will help us expand the reach of VoteforChange.com, so that more people can use this easy tool to find their early vote location and make sure their voice is heard," said Obama spokesman Nick Shapiro.[17]

Here's how the in-game advertising worked: The video game console connects to the Internet, so it can be updated with new features, including ads. As and example, "Burnout: Paradise," the game came out in stores in January of 2008, but the Obama ads were inserted many weeks later via "updates" in the game as it was hosted on Xbox Live servers. Xbox Live subscriptions can be free or paid for, depending upon the level of service, but credit-card information gives Microsoft details about where

---

[17] http://www.foxnews.com/story/2008/10/15/obama-campaign-buys-ads-in-18-video-games.html

each subscriber lives, allowing it to send regionally targeted ads to each individual.[18]

The following are some of the main areas where virtual reality is already being used in adverts and marketing:
- Sports and entertainment: mountain hiking is in the forefront of using the virtual reality technology. This enables the users to hike over mountainous regions and other dangerous paths. A virtual reality software called Trailscape, developed by Merrell during the of Capra [a hiking boot] was largely accepted.
- Hotels and hospitality: an innovative idea was presented by Marriot Hotels Group which allows prospective clients and users to have a virtual honeymoon displaying a simulated feature of their hotel facilities and services. In the experiment, newly married couples in New York City were asked to test the device and have a taste of the experience. Most of the respondents had exhilarating experiences, looking forward to the real environment
- Automobile: In 2014, Volvo launched virtual reality in its advertising campaign of the XC90 Luxury SUV. This was made in partnership with VFX studio. Prospective buyer can take a test-drive over different terrains while still in the comfort of his room. In 2016, Audi presented cars in their showrooms using the HTC Vive.
- Shopping: in November 2016, CNN reported the introduction of virtual reality by Alibaba that makes buyers have a more immersive experience of the products they are purchasing. Experts are already forecasting that by 2050, virtual reality may have replaced more than 60% of street shopping. This will be a period where orders can be placed and items bought through your virtual device and robot drones will do the delivery.

---

[18] Ibid

Other companies already using virtual reality are Amazon, Ikea, eBay Australia and Gatsby.

In the near future, people will be able to visit a fashion virtual fashion shop, with the clothing well rendered and can be tested on. this will be mutually beneficial for both buyers and sellers. The seller can showcase his brand in its entirety by packaging the brands music, branding signs, image of store and so on in a well package virtual reality experience for the buyer.

Consequently, buyers, in less time can experience the totality of a brand within seconds. Inspect more items from a 360-degree VIRTUAL reality experience. They can easily sift through their needed categories thereby improving satisfaction. Other indirect advantages will be the reduction in the need for parking spaces, conveniences and physical customer care needs. Shopping will be more secured, less stressful and fun. The actualization of all these will completely revolutionize the way shopping has been experienced prior to now.

Some additional markets that will be disrupted by virtual reality:

Adult Entertainment: Adult entertainment is widely acknowledged as one of the most powerful drivers in the development of the Internet. From the beginning, it led to pioneering improvements in streaming video, online payment systems, and other features of e-commerce. Now the industry is turning its focus to virtual reality and is again proving to be one of the principal engines of the spread and further innovation of this technology. The following charts created in 2018, show the tremendous force both economic and exposure (no pun intended) that adult entertainment brings to the industry.

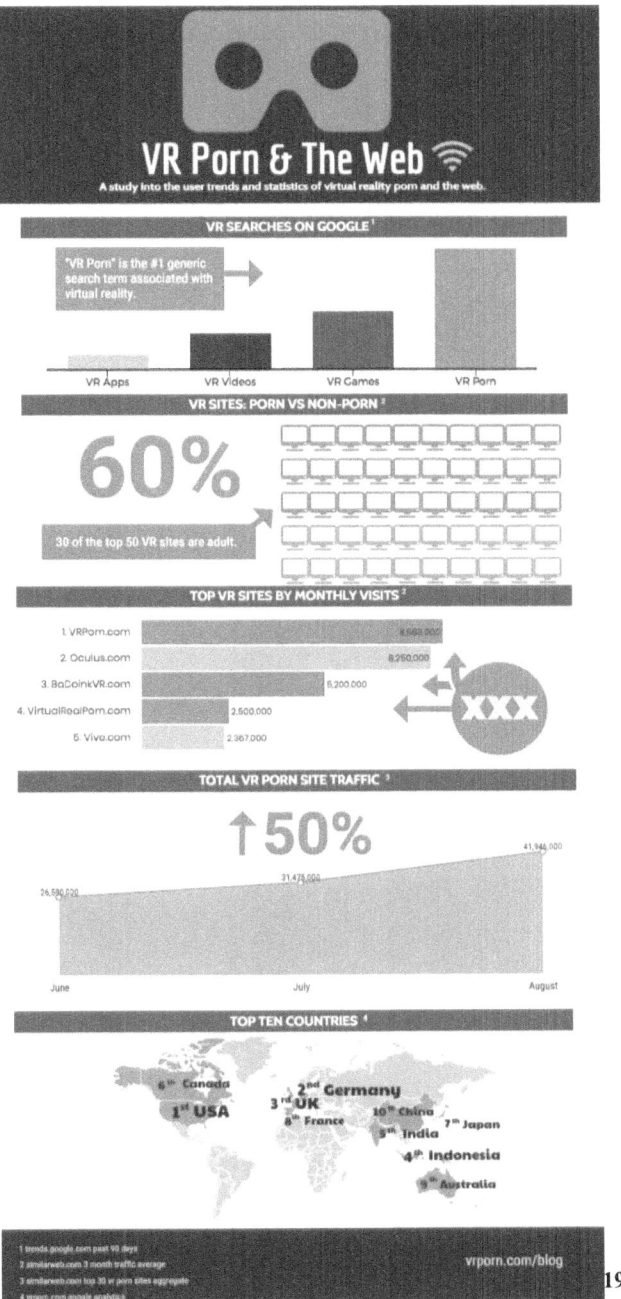

[19] https://bigthink.com/paul-ratner/the-future-of-vr-will-be-shaped-by-the-pornography-of-today

Fine arts: Some critics and fans have expressed concerns that virtual reality may negatively affects fine arts. But there are several exhibits that currently show how virtual reatlity is actually complimenting it. Many art museums are now changing the ways they do presentations and exhibitions. At the Jewish Museum in New York, Pierre Chapeau did a virtual reality exhibition of the works of Dillie Scofidio & Renfro. There are problems and rewards for the technology in this field. According to Deepa Mann-Kler, artist and founder of Neon, "I get the feeling a lot of creative people are blindsided by how much technology can allow now. It's a completely new language and one that we're only just beginning to find our feet with. We need to be out of our comfort zone, working in multidisciplinary teams – creating, prototyping and testing, and going through that cycle.

"VR is already showing up in museums – the Tate Modern did an exhibit with Modigliani and HTC Vive. But what are the implications?

"I love VR, but I have issues with the fact [that] half your face is covered and it's a solo experience. It's also a really expensive medium. The Tate exhibit was very expensive to produce. For laypeople, it can be confusing, all these different headsets. Phone-less headsets are very important developments. But why is it still worth it?"[20]

Architecture and Urban Planning: from designing to presentation of designs to client, virtual reality is taking in very dynamic position in planning and architecture. Design software systems are now designed considering the change in the interface of the software and the user. The mouse and keyboard are being replaced with the designer's hands, where he can use his hands in modelling his buildings and creating spaces. This of

---

[20] https://www.siliconrepublic.com/machines/virtual-reality-arts-qub

course will be in addition with the HMD (Head Mounted Device).

The virtualized drawing techniques will aim to link simulation and visualization through gestural modelling. With this, the issue of scaling in design will no longer be an issue as what is modelled virtually is not a mere representation of the real building or space, but the model in the actual sense of physicality.[21]

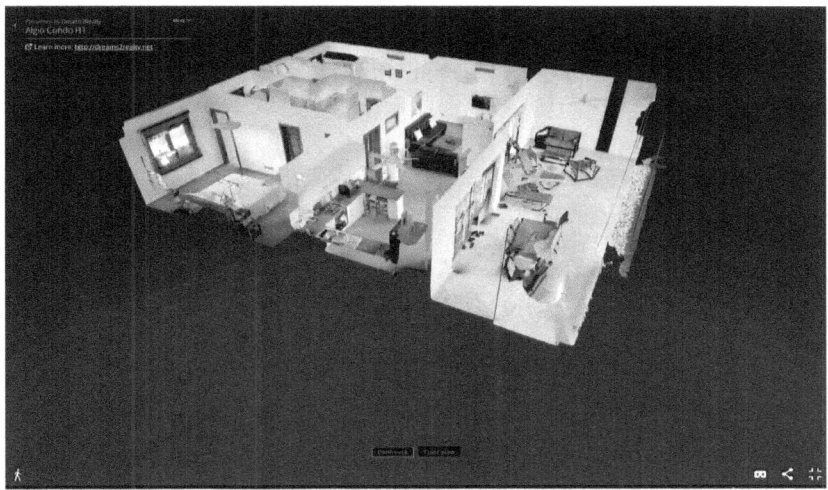

For presentations, clients will have access to a walkthrough experience, where they will experience true scale and photorealistic rendering. Also, architects are also able to use the Google Photosphere app as a 360 panorama photo apps to simulate construction sites that can be used by clients, consultants and contractors.

Virtual reality will enhance the abilities of architects, planners and clients. With the in real world terminal of the virtual reality model, a building or environment can be re-modelled and also experienced by the user, prior to construction. When the technology is made simpler, home users can use the terminal for visualizing in making changes in the buildings such as change in paint, landscaping and so on, enabling them to make a better-informed decision.

---

[21] www.glarimedia.com

Real Estate: With over 80% of all domestic buyers researching homes online, clients are wading through thousands of identical annoying online images and reading through spec sheets ad nauseam, realtors recognize that VR is quickly becoming one of the most powerful methods of promotion and client attraction. VR is on the verge of exploding into the mainstream and becoming a multibillion dollar platform. One-third of all buyers, and 41% of Millennial buyers, purchased properties they had not stepped foot into. -76% of real estate professionals surveyed stated they are currently, or plan on using Virtual Reality in 2017 - Studies show 95% of a message is retained in from a video source compared to only 10% from a text based message - Using VR and properly marketing a property has been shown to add 1.77% to the final sale price of a property. (additional $3,540 for a $200K sale)[22]

[23]

---

[22] https://www.amazon.com/Virtual-Reality-changing-Estate-Market-ebook/dp/B073TCSCGP/ref=sr_1_1?ie=UTF8&qid=1538973791&sr=8-1&keywords=how+vr+is+changing+real-estate

[23] www.glarimedia.com

24

In addition, architects and interior designers can use virtual environments to avoid costly remodel mistakes, and to show possible financial backers.

Engineering: Virtual reality helps engineers to gain a better understanding of their designs in a more encompassing 360-degree- 3D format. In addition to this is the higher probability of detecting potential flaws, risks, imperfections and danger in the design. These potentials risks can also be observed within a safe environment with no danger involved.
25

---

[24] www.glarimedia.com

[25] https://www.youtube.com/watch?v=wvmipZ3PHUY

Engineering fields such as rail construction and structural designs are two of those already taking advantage of the technology, from the design concept, prototyping, implementation and construction stages.

Military: The army, navy and air force are gradually adopting virtual reality for the training soldiers on dangerous terrains without the risks of injury and death. The soldiers are made to wear head-mounted displays and data gloves. Life-threatening situations can be simulated in a controlled environment to develop the competence of the soldiers and how they can cope with life-daring circumstance. increased combat capabilities have been reported when soldiers are exposed flight and battlefield simulations.

Beside the advantage of risk prevention, virtual reality has an additional advantage of cost saving. Generally, military trainings (and more especially flight trainings) are extremely expensive. Virtual reality simulations of the trainings is immensely less expensive and studies have shown that the outcome of the training on the soldiers is impressive. Other uses of the Virtual reality in the military include vehicle simulation, virtual boot camps, and medic training.

Automotive manufacturing: car designs are now first done in virtual reality before actual manufacturing. The period between design and production has now been shortened because designs are made early in the process of design. Automotive manufacturers like Ford and General Motors use virtual reality not just in the design process, but also to test for tolerances, and examine safety during the early stages of the design. Processes that would have taken months before can easily be completed within few days.

For example, with the CAVE software, automotive engineers can visualize the vehicle being designed in a real-world scale, evaluating the features and design qualities, ensuring the vehicle is both aesthetically pleasing and technically functional.

Aviation and aeronautics: For many years, flight simulators have been used in the aviation industry. virtual reality has been used in simulating cockpits. A leading virtual reality software in the industry is the Bohemia Interactive Simulator which combines D-BOX motion seats with a head-mounted display and Leap Motion controllers. This is used in training pilots and other flight crew members. The trainings are done in real-time, the experiences well controlled and the outcomes of the experiences can be better documented. With virtual reality, trainings cheaper, more affordable and more easily accessed. Also, because virtual reality trainings can be controlled as desired, it engenders faster learning and assimilation. When combined with augmented reality, the result is extremely impressive. skills transfer is faster, knowledge retention is easier and competence is better evaluated.

Apart from flight training, Virtual Build, used in aircraft design, has impacted positively in the creation of flight workspace, and process ergonomics. The simulations show designers more efficient ways to reduce unnecessary travel paths in manufacturing, eliminating discomfort and injury by giving adequate clearance reviews, and achieving more qualitative assembly procedures.

Occupational Safety and Health: it has been discovered that virtual reality trainings has more than 90% retention rate with no physical risks as obtained in real world. Fields such mining, aviation, military, construction, crime and disaster-response are harnessing the safety advantages of virtual reality in achieving good outcomes.

An example in construction is the design and installation of electrical fixtures and fittings. According to the US National Institute of Occupational Safety and Health, the electrocution rate was 12.2 per 1 million full-time construction workers in the 2011. This was even as much as nine times higher in other industries combined. This translated to a loss of almost $950,000 per person, taking into consideration medical costs and cost due to delayed work.

With the advents of virtual reality, such cases of electrocution have reduced. Even in the areas of fire-fighting training and services, remarkable progress is being made. VIRTUAL

REALITY trainings through its immersive, engaging and interactive capabilities, employed in constructability process and training facilities are increasingly acceptable and productive.

Courtroom and Judicial systems: Virtual courtrooms are now being created by the Virtual and Augmented Reality. This is to replace the traditional courtrooms. The judges, counsels, court staffs and witnesses will be interacting in this virtual courtroom, made secured by the cloud-based service of devices such as Oculus and HTC Vive. This is expected to make the judicial process faster, more cost effective, safer and easier. Witnesses can be cross-examined from any location, judges, lawyers and prosecutors can handle more cases and everything is being recorded in real time.

During the court proceedings, exhibits can easily be submitted and accessed by the required parties. Just imagine if a judge, through the use of a head-mounted device can 'enter' a crime scene, it will greatly reduce or even eliminate confusion in crime scene description. Presently, some researcher at Durham University are developing a robot called MABMAT that can capture the 3D view of a crime scene and convert it into a viewable material in virtual reality.

Kitchen Sink Studios have recently shown capability of recreating crime scenes by merging information gotten from victims' stories, police reports and witness accounts. The visual is created in the mode viewable by a head-mounted Device. Usually the Virtual movies is less than 30 seconds in duration. These, no doubt will create more enabling environment for jurors to examine facts thoroughly and thereby giving better judgements.

CHAPTER 7
AUGMENTED REALITY VS VIRTUAL REALITY

Augmented reality is the real-time overlay of the real environment with computer-generated audio, visual, graphical and hepatic feedbacks. It may also be referred to as computer-mediated reality. With such overlay with digitally generated inputs, the perception the real world is enhanced and augmented. This superimposition diminishes the difference between the real and virtual worlds.

[26]

While virtual reality creates a completely artificial environment, augmented reality on the other hand digitally overlays the existing real environment with additional information on it. Both has the giving a user an immersive experience. With augmented reality, the users is able to keep in touch with the real world while in a virtually simulated environment, while in the case of virtual reality, the user is isolated from the physical environment. In fact, for virtual reality, the more isolated, the better.

---

[26] https://www.electronicdesign.com/industrial-automation/brave-new-augmented-reality-awaits

Currently the capabilities of virtual reality works better in video games and for social interaction in a simulated environment. Based on general application, virtual reality seems to be ahead of augmented reality. There is now a significant rise in AR devices such as Glass from Google and other AR manufactures. Cell phone apps seem to be leading the way with AR adoption. Games like Pokeman Go introduced the masses to AR, and changed how many in business and marketing think of AR. "In the year since its release, Wadelton claims that "the success of Pokemon Go has shown artists, developers and programmers that AR content can prove to be a riveting success," although whether Pokemon Go will be emulated anytime soon remains to be seen. He adds: "It's shown that AR content can prove successful with mass audiences, and bring financial rewards to a company."[27]

Both AR and VR possess far greater impact that what we are currently seeing. Both will eventually be successful. Some experts are of the opinion that augmented reality may enjoy more success because it does not entirely isolate a user from his natural environment. Other researchers are of the opinion that virtual reality may do better because it has the ability to give full immersion and make the artificial become real, while augmented reality still leaves the user with the experience of the real world.
In all, we are now living in an era where anything is possible, where a new definition of what we know as reality is evolving, and both augmented and virtual realities will play a major role.

In the preceding chapters, we have discussed virtual reality from its inception, to the present day. In the next few sections we will

---

[27] https://www.thedrum.com/news/2017/07/07/did-pokemon-go-really-change-how-marketers-view-augmented-reality

examine the possibilities of virtual reality from a technical standpoint, but also from a moral and ethical standpoint.

CHAPTER 8
WHEN VIRTUAL REALITY MEETS ARTIFICIAL INTELLIGENCE

We are starting to understand artificial intelligence as a very interesting and highly impactful emerging technology. But what is artificial intelligence? Artificial intelligence is the term used to refer to any device or machine that possess and displays cognitive functions that human minds possess. It is what enables such devices to carry out activities such as learning and problem solving. Many companies are seeing the benefits and profits that AI can provide. Here is a chart showing the dollars being spent.

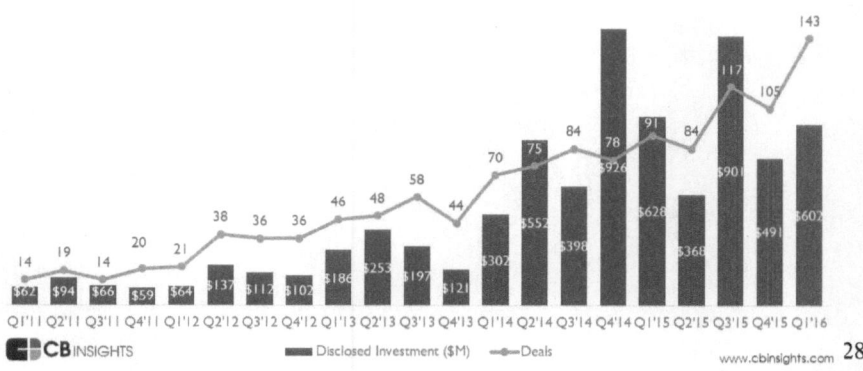

[28]

As machines becomes more complex, activities such as the recognition of optical character that were once thought to be artificial intelligence are now common technology. In today's world one of such activities that could still be referred to as artificial intelligence is the understanding of the human speech. In the study of artificial intelligence, researchers believe that intelligence, as the central quality of a human being can be described, studied and therefore simulated by a machine. That is why it has also been described as the science, technology and engineering of making intelligent machines.

---

[28] https://www.weforum.org/agenda/2016/06/investors-are-backing-more-AI-startups-than-ever-before

Presently the main research areas for AI include natural language processing, planning, learning, knowledge, perception, reasoning and the ability to manipulate and move objects. Knowledge is being drawn from several fields including neuroscience, computer science, mathematics, psychology. Philosophy, linguistics and many more.

Both virtual reality and artificial intelligence are going to change our perception of the world as we know it today. Everything will no longer seem the way it naturally is anymore. If both ever achieve their maximum potential, man would have conquered most of his own limitations. Artificial intelligence is now used in manufacturing to reduce human errors through virtual reality technologies.

In the past, the advancement of artificial intelligence experienced many setbacks due to ethical and philosophical reasons. Nevertheless, is is gradually being incorporated into such fields as healthcare, automotive, finance and video games. Even in security, both are now able to the identify the image and personality through artificial intelligence reported via virtual reality display. Also, in sales, virtual showrooms will help buyers select better.

There are three categories of artificial intelligence. These are strong AI, weak AI and normal AI. Those that fall into the group called strong AI strive towards developing machine that will reason and act in the same way as human do. The second group simply develop AI based on self-determined patterns. The third group called the weak AI, simply focus simply uses the human reasoning as a model to guide their research, the mimic of the patterns of human reasoning is not their final aim.

On the other hand, the study of virtual reality has allowed us to have improved virtual environment. Through an improved virtual environment have helped in creative highly immersive 3D simulated environments, enhancing collaboration, interaction and better feedbacks.

A successful combination of virtual environment and artificial environments has given birth to what can be referred to as virtual intelligence. This is the what emerges by the intersection of the two technologies.

Many of the world's biggest businesses including retail, gaming, healthcare and even gaming are already making vital changes to the way they do business by incorporating artificial intelligence and virtual reality. On this, Facebook seems to be at the forefront of utilizing these two technologies. Mark Zuckerberg, its CEO believes that these technologies will provide users with a more thrilling and qualitative social media experience beyond what it is currently doing now.

The hope is hat in the future, Facebook will include 360-videos and also include contextual updates. With artificial intelligence, objects in an image can be better explained, and speech will be better understood.

Major players such as Google and Amazon have introduce AI into the home as "Digital Assistants" Amazon trailblazed with their "Alexa" and Google quickly follow suit with a competitor.

"One of the numerous offshoots from Google AI is its improved Google Assistant. With Assistant, Google AI can process commands from a user, make phone calls silently in the background and handle natural conversation to request information or book appointments.

Amazon Alexa   Google Hue

Some critics are reserved or opposed to the directions Google, and other companies are taking with AI. Because the Assistant software does not declare itself as a digital assistant, critics say it deceives answering parties who may not wish to speak to an AI. Privacy is also a concern with Google's AI updates. For example, because Assistant no longer requires users to say "OK, Google" to alert the Assistant before issuing commands, critics argue that this change could enable constant data mining."[29]

Also, the retail industry, in their use of smart mirrors in the dressing rooms have also started positively in the embrace of the artificial intelligence technology. A further exposure to machine learning and better simulations via the virtual reality devices, the will have a better capacity to offer more unique and personalized services to their customers. The retailer, North Face, have developed a tool called Fluid Expert Personal Shoppe, powered by Watson, which opens up its customers to a more personalized search experience.
Visual Listening is another field of artificial intelligence that uses algorithms to study image-sharing platforms like Pinterest or Instagram, to give a better understanding about users are sharing concerning their brand.

---

[29] https://whatis.techtarget.com/definition/Google-AI

CHAPTER 9
VIRTUAL REALITY AND THE CHANGING WORLD OF BUSINESS

It is eventually going to be "The virtual world of business". As we speak, many business and corporations are already engaging virtual reality as an effective way of achieving affordability developing services and products. As manufacturers are making VR headsets, more available and affordable, so are the organization maximizing the opportunities in their businesses. From virtual tours of a business environment, training of new employees and having a 360-degree view of buying a product, virtual reality is tremendously impacting the business world.
In the 2017 CES Trade Show, an unprecedented number of users who use virtual reality technologies were experienced. It was reported that there were about 271 exhibitors from more than 150 countries in the spaces allocated for augmented and virtual realities. And this is expected to be on the increase in subsequent years.
The world is accepting the virtual reality more by the day. According to Tim Baxter of Samsung Electronics America in the 2017 CES trade show, more than 5 million Samsung Gear VR headsets have been sold and that users watched more than 10 million hours of Gear VRs 360-degree videos. The following are some of the ways virtual reality is changing the face of business in the world today.

A new of Product/Service sampling:
Virtual reality has now created a new and more interesting way to promote their business. An example is the Lowe's Home Improvement in the U.S. which after designing their kitchens and toilets take prospective users through a virtual tour of the facilities, creating a thrilling and more immersive impression. Customers now have a better way to visualize and are more informed about their choices.

Alibaba is investing in VR and working on entire VR stores for their customers to shop in. See the below image as an artist's conception of what the experience would look like.

Higher Effectiveness in Product Creation

The more the virtual reality technology improves, it will soon be enabled to study the preferences of a user. When virtual reality gets to the stage where it can simulate the stimuli from all the five body senses, the feedback received from these stimuli can be used know the user's preferences and thereby be better positioned to creating products and services that meets his needs more adequately.

Paradigm Shift in Sales Strategy

The automotive industry are endearing buyers by allowing them have a taste of what they have to offer through a virtual ride. For example, the Audi VR experience uses ZeroLight's propriety software and visualization technology. The customers have the opportunity of experiencing their dream vehicle in real time in a virtual

---

[30] https://uploadvr.com/alibaba-vr-shopping/

environment., checking all the details and choosing their preferred accessories.

Expand the Tourism Experience

It is a really thrilling experience when you can pay a virtual visit to that choice tourist site, experiencing the fun while you are still in the confines of your room. With a VR Gear called VR boots, produced by Cerevo, virtual tourist will soon be able to feel the water and the sand on their feet as they take a stroll, while feeling the ocean breeze at the same time.

Tourism companies can now diversify their services from physical tourism to virtual tourism.

More Effective Training and Educational Programs

In the past, many job training programs have aspects with tasks that require hands-on learning that have not been thoroughly effective. But with virtual reality, these forms of knowledge and experience are better transferred and acquired by trainees. For instance, an air-conditioning and heating Training Centre based in Houston, Texas, in partnership with Brown Technical Media agreed to train students via the virtual reality medium. BTC will create the VR simulated course that is replica of the training centre's curriculum.

In a press release by the Brown Technical Media., that traditional training methods are fast are now being replaced by trainings by virtual reality media and that this is fast impact trainings in the technical fields just as virtual reality has over the years impacted medical training.

CHAPTER 10
EMERGING TRENDS FOR FUTURE VIRTUAL REALITY

Fully immersive virtual reality is now more likely to be here sooner than you expected. Although a lot has been achieved since when the concept of virtual reality emerged decades ago, we still seem to be merely scratching the surface.

Virtual Taste, Touch and Smell: the experience of virtual reality has been limited largely to the simulation of sight and sound. Some progress has also been made on the haptic (touch) senses. For virtual reality to be fully engaging, immersive and interactive the sense of taste and smell has to be incorporated. What if you can attend a virtual dinner where you will be served the best meal you have ever had. It will be an incredible experience. To achieve this, the three senses of touch, taste and smell will be made possible, in addition to sight (and sound) by merely putting on a virtual reality headset.

This is how it will work. Experts are now developing a bone conductor which acts as a transducer that has the capacity to simulate chewing. The eating or chewing sensations is transduced (or sent) from the wearer's mouth and ear drums using the bones and soft tissues as the vessels. the dining utensils will compose of gyroscopic equipment with sensors that simulates hand movement.

Project Nourished is a company that is exploring the possibilities that exist in futuristic eating. They are experimenting with virtual foods that can mimic taste and smell. This can be very helpful in helping people with sweet tooth in preventing sugar-related ailments.

Virtual machining: this is used for manufacturing of machine parts in a way that physical testing is not needed. This will consequently help in cost reduction, increased machine efficiency and increased speed in the manufacturing process. The parts are designed and produced virtually, errors are checked, virtual inspection like waviness and surface metrology can be used to check the simulated parts. Just as in manufacturing, the simulated production process can be used to increase the experience of new manufacturers.

Virtual globe: This is a 3D virtual software that simulates the earth surface in a 360-degree view. The user can experience a virtual navigation around the globe, observing both natural and man-made features such as water bodies, rocks, roads and buildings together with abstract features such as population. Virtual globe being developed further to being a faster and more convenient way find, distribute and visualize different types of data in a geographical context. The contents are also being developed to have a more immersive feel by enhanced haptic feedbacks.

In addition to developing the application for current simulations of the world, expert also intend using it for simulating the way the world is centuries ago, and how in can be millennia after now. This has been a very useful study tool for geographers, climatologists and archaeologist. Apart from private user, virtual globes are used in tourism, scientific research and disaster management.

Virtual globes are also very beneficial in teaching. Educators use it to help learners appreciate better the concept of space and geographical components.

Virtual human body: this is a virtual reality anatomical atlas. With it the interconnectivity between the various body parts can be virtually related with and understood. It allows for easy exploration of the human anatomy.

The virtual human body can be simulated to show the effects of some physiological or anatomical action on the physical body. For example, the effects of change of diet can be simulated and shown on the virtual body.

An extension to this application is is the interesting way by which the software can fast-forward in time to depict old age or go back in time to simulate how a person was decades ago. This will help greatly in the anatomical and physiological study of the human body organs, simulating their conditions and thereby making it easier for diagnosis.

Mixed Reality: this (also known as MR or Hybrid Reality) is the result of the dynamic integration of both virtual and augmented realities, producing a new environment where real and simulated environments interact in real time. Sometimes in can be made to operate in a continuum which covers a range of experiences from a completely real environment to a totally virtual environment.

Its applications range from the entertainment industry to education, business and manufacturing fields. For instance, in education, MR is used foe Simulation Based Learning (SBI). This is a gradual shift from e-learning to what is now referred to as s-learning. With this, better knowledge sharing and assimilation can be more effectively achieved.

It will also give a increase to a more effective remote working. Saving in the stress and cost of commuting and also reducing the cost of rendering services. This is possible because of the immersive and collaborative environment that will be simulated for the workforce, simply by a head-mounted device. Other fields of use include aviation and healthcare.

Extended Reality: usually referred to as XR. It is a relative new concept in the technology world. It is the combination of all technologies involving virtual, augmented, and mixed reality. It is a technology which will allow a user to switch or translate easily from real to virtual worlds and back seamlessly without any form of boundary.

The XR terminology emerged as the distinction lines between virtual, augmented and missed realities are getting more blurry and indistinguishable by the day. Presently, companies such as Khronos (which developed Open XR cross platform), Pixvana, Nvidia and Oculus are already visualizing XR as an umbrella that can cover all three aspects.

In the nearest future, experts are envisioning a simple wearable XR device that can be worn like an eye glass that will combine the capabilities of a smartphone, a VR head-mounted device and an AR glasses, all in one. This mobile will even have the capacity to replace the TV, the PC and many other visual-based gadgets, creating an extremely immersive, and cognitive experience.

In fully enabling XR to revolutionize the technology world, it will need to go far beyond just creating a device that is sleek and comfortable. The display should be enabled to switch seamless between transparency and opacity, and between reality and virtuality. This will be in addition to a higher frame rate, increased resolution and a much wider field of view.

CHAPTER 11
ANTICIPATED IMPACTS OF EMERGING 3D VIRTUAL REALITY

The world wide web has undoubtedly changed the face of technology over the last few decades. But some industries have more impacted than others. Some industries, though impacted, have not been able to maximize the full potentials of the web. Real estate is an example of an industry that has been impacted by the internet. This is due to 2-dimensional quality of the internet, where you can only interact with the monitor of your compute or the screen of your mobile device. These are all flat interfaces. The interactive 3D interface of the virtual reality technology sets it apart.
The following are some of the ways, virtual reality is expected to better impact us in the nearest future:

Internet and Personal computers: nowadays, virtual reality device are empowered with higher pixel resolution. And the this will continue for a long time, till virtual reality is as immersive as actual reality. Oculus and HTC Vive now runs on a pixel resolution of 2160x1200. This places a huge demand on the graphics hardware of our PCs. Future realism is aiming at an 8K resolution. And even further to holographic displays. The demands getting higher and the pressure is getting more on the computer CPU.
In response to this, companies like Nvidia and AMD have developed the softwares called "Virtual Reality works" and "Liquid virtual Reality" respectively which performs image warping. To achieve full immersion, these companies may need to change the fundamental principles guiding the production of virtual reality chips to meet future demands.
Same applies to the internet. With virtual reality, the volume of information available on the internet will multiply several times over. It will be something unprecedented. Information and websites will be configured and displayed in a totally different way. No one is certain yet, on the dimension this will take. But

one thing is sure, it will change how people use the internet. That is why the future era of the internet is being described as the internet of experience.

Mobile devices and accessories: With extremely enhanced design and head-tracking capabilities, the virtual reality technology nowadays has achieved extensive results. you're all set to go.

Soon every smart phone will be VR-enabled. This will further open up the virtual world, making mobile VR experiences cheaper and available. Immersive VR will go popular not on laptop computers, intelligent TVs or Nintendo wii but on smartphones.

Affordable HMDs such as New Samsung Gear VR and Google Daydream View are already synchronizing with early adopters for VR game playing and content streaming through applications such as Netflix VR and HBO. But this is just the beginning. With mobile VR, companies can create amazing live and VOD viewing experiences for customers to watch on their smartphones, using a variety of movie types (e.g. 2D, 3D, 180/360 degree).

Education and Learning: Technology and education are inter-related. Unfortunately, both have not been complimentary as expected. The UNESCO Institute of Statistics has expressed concerns that at at the end of year 2016, there are no fewer than 263 million children in the world that are not involved in any form of primary education. Even in the secondary schools more than 5.1 million teachers will be needed before 2030. The gap between learning needs and available school in increasingly worrisome. But virtual reality seems to have the answer in providing not only quantitative education, but also a qualitative learning environment.

- Tutors can reach more learners: since it will be a virtual class, supported by the internet, a teacher can reach tens of thousands or even millions of learners at the same time. Classroom distractions will be more controllable and learning

services better coordinated. The ever-widening gap the demand for learning and the supply of schools can be better closed.
- Learning becomes easier and even more interactive: students can have a real classroom experience when they are physical in the comfort of their home. Same with tutors. Both of them can better schedule their interactive session, done in a relaxed location and atmosphere. Time and stress of commuting to school, will be eliminated.
- Inspiration for Creative Learning: in contrast to traditional learning, virtual reality will stimulate imagination, a learner will not only view what is being describe but can relate to the environment. Also, complex concepts and theories, when better simulated, will be better understood.
- Creates learning experiences with less resources: with virtual reality, students will be able to go on a tour or field trip without leaving the comfort of their homes or classes. This will eliminate travelling and commuting risks, logistics and expenses. Kids have been said to learn more from experiences than in reading. With virtual reality the field trip learning experience can be controlled, removing travelling excesses of over-eating, wanderings and distractions. A good example of this is the software called The Giza Project which takes the user back through time, exploring the Pyramids, without stepping into the North African country.

Passive learning becomes a thing of the past: learning becomes more active and distractions are limited or totally excluded because of the immersive nature of Virtual reality. Users are engaged in the virtual environment since their senses have been engaged by the medium. Educators have long known that different people learn better in different ways. Some people learn by listening, some by watching and other need to actually touch or interact. Virtual reality will be able to engage and incorporate all styles and maximize the quality of the educational experience.

Businesses and the Economy: Virtual reality and augmented reality is fast changing the way people view business reality and the economy. The following are some of the expected contributions of virtual reality in the business and economic spheres in the next couple of years.
- **Prototyping and project simulations**: Organizations will be better enabled to visualize a product, yet to be manufactured, by simulating what they will build at conception stages and thus provide more effective feedback earlier in the process, reducing time and resources that would otherwise have been wasted.
- **Presentations and Proposal Presentation**: Power point presentations are now being embedded in virtual reality. documentation and presentations of business proposals will be made more real.
- **Staff recruitment**: A recruiter will have a better interaction and assessment of a job applicant. Applicants on the other hand can better express their competence.

With virtual reality, distance is no longer a barrier in conducting an interview with full sense of user presence. This is nothing compared to what Skype has to offer. With the HMD, both the interviewer and the candidate can have the experience of being present in the same location.
In addition to this, virtual reality will enable prospective candidates make more better decisions in job selection. He can explore the office and even get to meet existing staff without physically going to such organization. This will have a long-term effect reducing employee turn-over.
In addition, collaboration will be improved. Information that can be perceived and translated by all the body senses can be transmitted in real time and feedback is received immediately.
General Mills, the famous food company uses the Oculus Rift in recruiting. During the interview process, the company takes the interviewee through a tour around the General Mills Golden Valley campus. Also, in 2015, Jet started using

Samsung's VR for interviews in its New York City Headquarters. Same applies to German company Deutsche and the Commonwealth Bank of Australia, to mention but a few.

Larger Demand and Supply in the Economy: customer/clients will have better interaction with the salesman/professional, products are services are better marketed by a greater number of persons and hence increase the demand and supply of goods and services through increased virtual presence. The virtual reality medium will become a more effective way to assess a product or service and hence drive the market. Some examples that experts envision:

Medicine and Healthcare:

- **Therapy**: Although Virtual Reality Exposure Therapy has been used over the years, it has not gained much popularity due to some technological limitation and affordability issues. The production of virtual reality HMD has solved these problems to a large extent, making greater access to mental health by patients. Exposure and cognitive behavioral therapies are now taking the advantage of virtual reality technology to create a more controlled environment.
An impressive development of a virtual reality software solution for Post-Traumatic Stress Disorder [PTSD] which relieves anxiety and stress in patients that have undergone some traumatic experience. It combines the task of eye movement and memory recall to make the traumatic experience less clear.
In the future, asides PTSD, virtual reality therapy will be become more potent in treating phobias. Examples of software that will emerge better in couple of years are: Virtually Better, Psious, VirtualRet, Mimerse. The software companies are developing their capacity to treat such patients with phobias of flying, heights, blood, public spaces and public speaking.
Although there has been long term research on the use of virtual reality for mental therapy, but this has not full penetrated the market. Extensive research is still ongoing on

the long-term safety of these types of software. The more data researchers are able to provide on their safety, the more it will be acceptable to healthcare givers

Health safety: fear of contacting an infectious disease will be in a general space will be doused. For instance, if colleague or classmate have a flu, you won't be afraid to meet with the person in a virtual world.

- **Medical and paramedic training**: a virtual reality software called "We Are Alfred' created and further developed by the company, Embodied Lab uses the virtual reality technology to teach young medical doctors what it means to be a 74-year-old man. While in the simulated environment, the young doctors' physical abilities were aged, similar to that of an elderly. Impairments in audio-visual capabilities were incorporated. This training was used to improve the empathy shown by caregivers to aged persons.
- **Preventive Medicine**: immersive "cafe style" systems can be used to discourage people from negative and health-deteriorating lifestyles. A lot of research is still being done on the most effective patterns of virtual interactions and storyboards on people.
- **Dentistry**: through the the use of the software called HapTEL, new dentists are being trained to carry out dental procedures like filling using a pressure drill. The interesting part of this is that the software simulates the pressure and movement needed to carry out this operation.
- **Spatial Design of Health Care Facilities**: in the construction of healthcare facilities, architects, designer and health practitioners have the opportunity to experience a building even while at the conception stage. This reduces or even eliminates construction errors, cost and time. The healthcare givers also feel more involved in the design process.

Through the Head-mounted devices of Oculus Rift and HTC Vive, the users are fully immersed into the environment, and healthcare giver can even see and experience such spaces as theatres, wards and consulting rooms, way ahead before construction commence.

Distance Medicine: With the shortage of healthcare professionals, virtual reality is allowing a single professional to be in multiple sites on a given shift. Rural hospitals are hiring online physicians as a way to combat shortages and higher costs. Some major hospital systems are using a single physician to triage critical care patients in multiple locations. With the help of virtual reality, these practices will become more effective and more widespread.

CHAPTER 12
CHALLENGES AND CONCERNS OF VIRTUAL REALITY ADOPTION

Virtual reality without a doubt is one of the promising components of future science and technology. It is changing the way people interact with devices and makes things that were formerly impossible to become reality. The impact and evolution of virtual reality technology will continue a long time into the future. Nevertheless, there have been concerns over the continuous technological advancements, acceptability and usage of the virtual reality technology that need to be examined no, and re-examined continuously going forward. Chief among these concerns are challenges are privacy, health/safety and philosophical concerns.

- **Privacy and Security**: Eric Muigner, a senior vice president at M&C Saatchi Mobile says that "Virtual reality platforms have the ability to collect unprecedented amount of data… that could be detrimental to the user's privacy". Asides from virtual reality's ability of gaining access to the user's location and web visits just like the internet does, it possesses the ability to study and save the users head and body movements, together with physical attribute of the individual. This creates a higher probability of identity theft.
Despite the enormous contributions of virtual reality, its ability to study, collect and store a huge amount of personal data poses both privacy and security risks. In view of this, future internet surveillance will of necessity need to adapt to the various privacy and security issues of virtual reality development, and ensure effective ways of dealing with them.
Another perspective beside using identity theft for criminal or "grey market targeting", is its use by marketers/manufacturers in tweaking advertisement to your specific needs. By receiving more in-depth information about you through the headset, it may be used by people who have such information to hyper target and develop marketing to sell to you products and services that they have predetermined you to need.

In addition to using personal identity information for advertisement purposes, there has been a growing concern on whether or not the data store through virtual reality devices can be used for state surveillance. For instance, Head mount devices has the capability to track your head movements, know where you are looking or facing and how you relate with your physical environment. Personal information like these can be used for surveillance even without the user's knowledge.

As with current technology, the question of how will my personal data be prevented from identity theft? How can a user be assured that the government (or possibly illegal-minded individuals) will not use their personal info to spy on me and disrupt their life? And how will third-party influences be controlled?

- **Health and safety**: Like any technology, virtual reality has side effects, despite its numerous positive impacts on the society. Although many of the health and safety side effect of virtual reality are temporary, it is a good idea for current users and prospective buyers to be abreast of such risks. Manufacturers are well aware of this, and that is why there are boldly-written health and safety warnings on the devices. Broadly these side effects can be grouped into three, namely: physical, psychological and physiological.

- **Physical Effects**: posture strain is a major physical health risk in virtual reality. Often, the postural demands of the user is abnormal while interacting with the virtual environment. The postural demands are as demanded by the task to be performed in the virtual environment.

    In addition to posture strain, the user is also at risk of what is called immersive injuries. When a user is on an fully immersive virtual reality device, he is deemed to be functionally blind to his immediate physical environment. The more immersive the user is, the more 'blind' he becomes. It must therefore be ensured that the user is limited to a protected area bounded by padded barrier in case of

accidental bumping. In newer devices, there are guidance systems built into such devices that alerts a user when the come close to the edge of the specified boundary.
- **Physiological Effects**: This seems to be the most well documented and researched health and safety challenge of virtual reality. The most common of these is cybersickness. This is sometimes referred to as virtual reality sickness. The symptoms which include nausea and headache occurs either during or after the use of the virtual reality device, especially the head-mounted displays. Based on recent research, studies are showing that cybersickness can me ameliorated by reducing the field of vision in the head mounted device.

  Another physiological concern is called the vergence-accommodation effect, which happens as the eyes strives to create a new convergence point inside the HMD as against creating a convergence point outside of it.

  Also worthy of mention is what has been referred to as Virtually Induced Motion sickness (VIMS). This is the conflict the body feels when the images in the virtual display signifies motion, whereas the balance organs of the body, and the non-vestibular organ indicates to the user that it is static and motionless. This occurs more in non-interactive virtual reality devices. It can also occur in fully interactive devices when the rate of body movement does not fully synchronize with that of the Virtual environment.
- **Psychological Effects**: virtual reality has the ability to create the illusion that the user can truly live in another sphere while still in his physical body. By extension, it may make an individual feel like he can own and therefore control another body. This has been referred to as depersonalization: where a long and constant experience of immersion in a simulated environment begins to make your body unreal to you.

  Generally speaking, at this time the physical and physiological effects of virtual reality are being understudied much more than the psychological effects.

  It is argued that as the technology becomes more "realistic" for the user, that general guidelines that are in place for video games now be examined. When the technology becomes seamless, will a user become desensitized to the experiences. Ethicisists are now exploring what guidelines should be enforced for virtual reality? Should "real world" rules be implemented such as whatever activity is not accepted by the society, should not be made into a virtual reality simulated experience. For example, games should not be made to allow users to shoot and kill people for fun when in reality, this will mean that a crime is being committed. The reason for this is simple: virtual reality is becoming more real, and the brain will easily adapt to what the simulated environment feeds it with. What safeguards are needed and what will the effects of such realistic environments be on the human brain is an area of study that is just now being explored with any urgency.

- **Philosophical and Ethical concerns**: Virtual reality can reframe a user's consciousness and moral state. since virtual reality manufacture can depict the kind of 'worlds' the desire by reflecting it in the simulated environments, this would mean that they will have the moral authority on the long-term behavioral options and patterns of the users. This will become dangerous if virtual reality providers depict a negative or morally-unhelpful environment.

The enabling of immoral and anti-societal acts like robbery, murder, grand theft, torture and rape in another ethical concern. with virtual reality, the world of these immoral acts will become more real to the user and philosophers and psychologist have opined that this may eventually result in physical crimes if not banned or at least censored.

Do the stakeholders of virtual reality industry have the moral duty to avoid negative contents on their mediums? Or at least shield it away from children and other more vulnerable groups? Research should leave no stone unturned in exploring the effects of such environments and the possibility of censoring or even banning harmful content in virtual reality. This is problematic in many ways for a "free speech" society, and presents an ethical dilemma for others to debate or at least in a different book.

CHAPTER 13
LIMITATIONS THAT NEED TO BE TACKLED FOR VIRTUAL REALITY ADOPTION

Stagnant Locus: One major limitation in the current 3D virtual reality is that it possesses only one POV. This means that use is restricted to the position created by the author. This happens especially when the content is crated with motion. The user remains in a fixed position and cannot possible view an object or element in a different position, other that the one made by the content creator. It is similar to the experience a fixed cameraman has, where he can view things from various angles in a hall and from a specified cone of vision, but his position remains fixed.

It is expected that in the nearest future, the viewer or user will be able to move and change position so that he can have seamless 360 experiences.

Cost: presently, virtual reality is still too expensive for most people. While the industry has scaled many hurdles and limitations over the past few decades, yet affordability remains a factor that has not been addressed.

While the prices are in a downward spiral, at the moment, if you want to have a good and high-end virtual reality experience, you might need between $1000-$2000 for the head mounted device and accessories for a PC virtual reality. You will need between $599 [for an Oculus Rift] and $799 {for an HTC Vive]. This is without the high-end computer system need, and this will be range of $1000.

For now, most virtual reality devices are high end devices and that is why they are costly. For future virtual reality to gain more momentum through affordability, there will be a need for not only high-end virtual reality devices, but also low and medium-based devices. With this, there will be range of prices and the industry with thrive better in reaching a wider customer base. Due to this need, Intel is already partnering with Microsoft to develop Windows 10-compatible virtual reality head mounted displays.

The partnership also includes many other computer-manufacturing company such as HP, Acer and Dell with a common goal of making devices with low PC spec requirements. The sooner investors create ranges of devices that can work with virtual reality, the more acceptable and affordable it will be.

A very good example of this was when Oculus introduced the Asynchronous Space warp together with its scalability features, the graphic performance requirement {and hence the cost] dropped by up to 40%.

Unconvincing realism: 3D virtual reality worlds are yet to be convincingly realistic because low resolutions, latency in motion tracking, limited field of view and they usually exhibit noticeable head motion lags. Also, is the fact that movable characters more often than not lack convincing details do not move naturally as it happens in the real world. This may be due to the adequate motion simulation that reflects forces of friction and gravity.

- Encumbering: as of today, most 3d virtual reality gadgets and tethers inhibit free body movement. This is especially true of virtual reality devices that uses assisted interactive technology. Until when these gadgets are sleeker, lighter and more compact, 3dvirtual reality will remain too bulky and encumbering.
- Health Concerns: presently, little is known about the long-term health risks 3dvirtual reality, probably due to the relative 'newness' of the technology, but there has been some documented short-term health and safety concerns. For instance, Oculus Rift's health and safety documentation list the following potential symptoms when the gadgets are used for more than 30 minutes at a stretch without intermittent break of between 10-15 minutes: eye strain, discomfort or pain in the head or eyes, muscle twitching, dizziness, disorientation, seizures, impaired balance, impaired hand-eye

coordination, excessive sweating, nausea, light-headedness, drowsiness, loss of awareness, and fatigue.
Currently virtual reality companies in the United States have started developing hardware that increases immerses and drastically reduces motion sickness among many other health challenges. The argument is that virtual reality and immersion is inversely proportional to motion sickness. The more realism you experience, the less motion sickness you are prone to having. Oculus and Crystal Cove are two major companies currently towing this line.

- Little or no ROI for investors yet: as at the second quarter of 2016, most investors in the 3D virtual reality market said their investments are yet to start yielding dividends. Most investors are projecting the year 2020 and beyond to start making noticeable returns on their investments if the popularity trend of the technology continues on rise.

CHAPTER 14
TOWARDS REALISM: CREATING BETTER VIRTUAL REALITY TECHNOLOGY WITH HIGHER IMMERSION AND SPATIAL PRESENCE

In creating a more convincing virtual reality that gives users a real-world simulation the following needs to be looked and made good enough in future (and even current) virtual reality technologies:

Low Latency: the lag time [or delay time] between the when a user initiates an action in the virtual reality device and when he gets a corresponding reaction from on the simulated environment is what is described as latency. Despite the advances in virtual reality technology, so much still needs to be done in creating devices with low latency, so the delay period action and reaction times will just be as in real time. Overcoming latency is one of the final challenges virtual reality will have to deal with. Currently the best of virtual reality devices, especially in the gaming industry operates with 50ms or even more. This is still gross high for a very real experience. Experts have suggested that a low latency of about 15 to 7ms motion-to-last-photons, combined with good prediction of head motions will be a considerably good starting point. Oculus Rift is now targeting as low as 30milliseconds in their dev kits. With low latency, the brain will be able to perceive the simulations as real. This is simply because the brain's perception will be unable to distinguish be difference between the real and unreal worlds. This may be hard with the current hardware configs we have around. But one thing is sure, if we want to get latency to be as low as even 7 milliseconds, then the industry has to step up and change the hardware rule.

Motion Tracking: this is the main intrinsic device in a virtual reality system. These devices or components interacts with the systems processing unit. This is what makes your view to shift when you move your head with a head-mounted device on. Your view in the virtual reality world changes as you tilt your head forward, backward, vertically or sideways. All tracking devices have one thing in common. They are made to percept six degrees of freedom within the x, y and z coordinates. The tracking system can either be electromagnetic, mechanical, optical or acoustic.

For better realism, the tracking must support translations in the x, y and z co-ordinates [called the roll, pitch and yaw coordinates, respectively] with a minimum of a millilitre accuracy. This gives adequate translations. In addition to this, the orientation should be at least of a quarter degree accuracy and a volume must be minimum 1.5metres on a side. There is presently no virtual reality device that possess these tracking configurations.

Optics: this is located in the head-mounted displays [HMD]. The HMD is an example of a near-eye display. It is one of the main interface between the user and the virtual reality device. However, the present generation HMDs are yet to have the capacity to produce fully natural optics that is both very real and comfortable. The reason for this is that, unlike natural vision the optical capabilities in the HMDs cannot fully replicate in focus. Also, they are yet to have the capacity of supporting users refractive eye defects.

Nevertheless, researchers are now making headway in this regard, by new computational optics technology with display modes that can conform to the users'. This will be achieved by using mobile gaze-tracking technology and lenses with tunable focus.

High Refresh rate: This rate, expressed in Hertz. It describes the number of times a display updates its content every second. It shows how often the display shows a new image from the general processing unit. Usually, the higher the refresh rate, the lower the latency. These days, most HMDs are 90 Hertz, and they are currently striving toward 120 Herts or more. This will enable a faster action-reaction interface thereby giving us lower latency.

Low Pixel Persistence: this is described as the amount of time it takes each pixel to remain lit. It is crucial to prevent the blurring of the eye motion and should not be more than 3 milliseconds to mimic reality. A higher persistence is more likely to cause smearing and eventual blurring of the images.

Wider field of view: this is the extent of the environment you can observe while in the virtual reality environment. The wider the field of view, the more immersion and presence you feel. The more, the better. There are two types of FOV: monocular and Binocular fields of view.
Monocular FOV describes the view for one eye. This ranges between 170-175 degrees between the pupil to the nose, and nasal FOV usually between 60-65 degrees for a normal healthy eye. Binocular FOV is the combination of the two monocular FOV for the two eyes. This ranges between 200-220 degrees. Where the two eyes meet, we have what is called a stereoscopic binocular FOV. This enables us to view things in 3D and is about 114 degrees.
In current virtual reality technologies, FOV range between 170-220 degrees. Despite this, the eyes still experience a visual phenomenon call tunnel vision caused by the HMD not able to fully capture the eyes' FOV as it would in the real world. The more the field of view the less the tunnel vision effect.

Adequate Resolution: resolutions describes the number of pixels in a display. The value is usually represented in width and height. For example, HDTV has a resolution of 1920 x 1080 [mostly depicted as 1080]. This means that it has a width of 1920 pixels and a height of 1800 pixels. if virtual reality is expected to give the same realism as the normal eyes perceive the real world, then resolution is key. A resolution of 1080p or more works well. There has been a challenge in resolution because of the wide FOV need.
Experts have said that for users to experience immersive virtual reality, at least a 4K resolution (3840x2160) must be achieved.

Palmer Lucky of Oculus Rift further stated that, for pixilation not to be noticeable by the eyes anymore, at least an 8K resolution (7680x4320).

CHAPTER 15 VIRTUAL REALITY: THE CAUTIONS

Of course, we have focused on the numerous advantages of virtual reality. What are the bad and ugly sides? Does virtual reality have negative impacts on our body and lives? What are the dark sides?

Addiction: the disconnection from real world and the immersive capabilities of virtual reality can create addiction. In May, 2016, Keith Ablow, a psychiatrist, in an article published in BBC news warned of the potential dangers in virtual reality. He explained that most internet contents like Facebook are like drugs that gives some sense of pleasure to the brain. It stimulates the pleasure contents of the brain, eventually making the user more psychiatrically ill.

The argument is that the more real and immersive the virtual reality technology becomes, the more its capacity to stimulate the pleasure centres of the brain, and hence the sickness. In the long run, a user may even suffer unpredictable mental challenges when withdrawn from the use of the device. As the virtual reality gets more immersive, a virtual life may be replacing the real life, depending on the level of addiction.

Escapism:
Virtual reality, when fully developed will not just be another way of experiencing reality, it will be another form of human consciousness. When a user is fully immersed in the simulated environment, his sense will not be fully aware of his surroundings. The user has temporarily escaped into an unreal world, when if not well managed can be a means where the user will neglect serious and tangible issues in the real world and slide into the simulated world of virtual reality.

This may not be so bad and could even be helpful for those who are naturally lonely or moody, but it becomes a problem when real-life roles and obligations are neglected due to uncontrolled access to virtual reality gadgets.

Motion sickness: This is most discussed topic when talking with adverse effects of virtual reality. Motion sickness is also known as travel sickness or kinetosis. It is the experience had when the perceived environment and the sense of movement of the vestibular systems are not in agreement. This has always been a phenomenon common to people since the era of boats and canoes. In the physical world, up to about 40% of persons experience this when they travel and the length of journey determines the severity. The most common symptoms are headache, stomach awareness, general discomfort, vomiting, nausea, sweating, fatigue. Drowsiness and disorientation. Since 2016, researcher have started confirming that indeed virtual reality headsets causes motion sickness. According to a survey carried out and published by ScienceNews Magazine, about 78% of women who use virtual reality headset constantly have complained about motion sickness, while 33% of the men experienced same.

Virtual Reality companies have claimed that motion sickness will be much reduced as the technology of the components of the device improves. That as the device gets more immersive and enters into a state where it is fully convinces the user's brain what it sees, hears and feel is real, the human senses send signals to the brain and the brain will in turn sends signals to the body to maintain the balance. The users and the virtual reality community can only wait to see how it pans out.

CHAPTER 16
CAN 'VIRTUAL REALITY' EVER BECOME 'ACTUAL REALITY'?

Many questions have been asked concerning virtual reality. Many are forward looking technologists are being asked; Can virtual reality be as real as the real world?

If so, how fast? How soon can virtual reality be made to capture our perceptions and stimuli through the five senses of human beings? Can virtual reality ever get to a point where it will be more preferable to the real world? So many questions yet to be answered about this ever expanding and changing field.
It is safe for us to believe that virtual reality can come very close to reality in the near future, so disrupting and forward looking

---

[31] https://io9.gizmodo.com/5276088/the-5-science-fiction-tales-that-made-us-love-virtual-reality

thinkers are already starting plan for it now. The advancements in the technology within a few decades leaves little doubt about its vast potential to be more immersive and user-consuming technology as the years roll by. Also, the involvement of successful and big companies such as Facebook, Google, and Oculus increases the probability of virtual reality. For example, ever since Facebook acquired Oculus, so much resources have been expended to make virtual reality truly a reality.

On the question of, "Can virtual reality can be more real than actual reality?" there are technical limits, for now, but the days are coming where such uses of the technology may arrive and we will have to decide what will the risk/reward payoff of adoption of such technologies. Some are already starting to predict that if this ever happens, there is the tendency of eventual, but gradual collapse of the social component of a humanity. Others say it will usher in a "Golden Age" of advancement and enlightenment". Virtual reality may be more fun and addicting in the long run when compared with the real world. Just imagine if you can take a dive from mount Everest without a parachute in the virtual reality world, enjoying the thrills with all your five senses without the fear of any imminent danger to your physical self.

This may be the point where we can, through advanced technology be able to taste, touch and even breathe in a virtual environment. This will be a stage closer to teleportation than we would ever have imagine. It will be an interesting way to escape reality. Virtual reality will bring more fun, but replacing actual reality can introduce entire new issues as a society. Great virtual reality can make you escape reality. But can it make you replace reality? Time will tell. There is more to the real world than fun and emotions.

CHAPTER 16
CAN 3D VIRTUAL REALITY SURVIVE THE FUTURE?

Virtual reality is gradually giving us a new perspective through which we can define what reality means. Before now, what is real has been construed as what exists it our physical and material. Reality is determined by external factors. But now, the definition of what is real depends on what our brain 'sees'. This next section is an exploration of how taking virtual reality to its extreme limits will affect society as a whole.

What if things like color, taste and smell are not properties of the outside world in itself, but simply a sense of simulation created by our perception?

The ability to experience another world, engaging all the body senses while physically in the real world is something that has been discovered to give pleasures to the brain. As long as the ability to stimulate the brain resides in virtual reality, inventors can always leverage on this, creating various media by which the pleasure can be further stimulated. With this logic, it is most unlikely that virtual reality may cease to exist. What may be dynamic are the devices and software that will be used as its platforms.

In addition to the above, another angle to look at this are the limitations of our natural physical bodies. Man has always dreamed of doing and achieve more than is ordinarily possible. Also, the human body is delicate. An unguided adventure can lead to serious physical injuries and even death. This has been the bane of many of man's wishes.

Many of our technologies have been aimed at making us to do more, but there are still vacuums left to be filled. Virtual reality has come to fill this vacuum. It is a bold step into dissolving many of the limitation we were born with. We can do virtually everything in a new way, devoid of physical risks and limitations.

In the future, of the ultimate aspirations of virtual reality that will be aimed at will be to create a virtual body, which is sometimes called an Avatar in a virtual world.
Let's paint the scenario of future virtual reality
Incredibly, your avatar's human body and feelings will actually be better than your natural feelings in many ways. For instance, your exclusive sight will have the same quality, however there will be no distortions from a biological stance, your eyes will not flicker, your sight will not go dim. Your muscles will be ideal - never exhausting - unless you modify the configurations so they do so. Your exclusive human body will be superhuman, ideal, and delightful. The virtual world will fit seamlessly with the virtual human body. It will be more than real than you think
Think about, for example, looking at a grassy area in a sport. As you move onto the area it will be ideal. Each blade of grass will be completely established. It will have no fresh weeds, no divots, it will be perfect. You will be able, if you wish, to take your outfits off and move on to this ideal lawn. It will feel just like lawn in every sense. But this is a virtual environment, so if you want it one millimeter wider or a change to a slightly different color of green, the modification is immediate. you can modify the type of the lawn, the wetness content, the ground beneath it, even add fresh flowers if you want. To your thoughts, your experience, the lawn will be completely actual because the sensations of experiencing the grass are streaming straight through the brain's natural neurological sensors programs.
The same will be true of every in-game atmosphere you experience. Run through a woodland. Ski down a hill. Walk through a complete re-creation of London. Walk on the celestial satellite. Swimming along a totally simulated reefs offshore. But in addition, you will be able to do things that your actual human body cannot possibly do now. Fly through the air like a super hero. Drive a flying carpet. Be part of the gunfight at the OK Corral… and then respawn to do it again.
With "Vertebrane" (Avatar) software, you will be able to check out any simulated location immediately - even unreal planets. You will also have the option of going to different times as well

as different places. You will be able to fly, be present at any traditional moment, be rich without limit, be as wonderful as you want, die and be born-again, eat anything you like in any amount, or just sit on a exotic seaside and sunbathe alongside a pool - all without ever making home! In short, you can be anyone and do anything you like. You can select to have these encounters with your loved ones, or with synthetic people, or simply alone. The entertainment industry is starting to churn out entertainment depicting such lifestyles at an ever-increasing rate.

Given the choice of being in your actual human body vs. your virtual body, you will select your virtual body most of the time. Therefore, your real-life human body will not so real anymore. It is conceivable that at some point technology will evolve to the point where it will become possible to discard your human body and have only your thoughts located some form of in a technological brain storage service and be linked with a directly connected-type PC as portrayed in popular movies such as 'The Matrix". Here, along with a large number of other minds, you will be reduced to the sum of your thoughts and will be wrapped in a safe, liquid-filled life-support area.

This will eliminate all of the hazards that come along with having a human body. It will also significantly increase durability by keeping the ecological conditions constantly at ideal levels and eliminating almost all hazards of your past lifestyle. Of course, such a storage would have to feature the highest possible security, strengthened structures, resistant to quakes, tornados, tanks, etc. A totally different definition of "life", all brought about by the extension of the technology that we see starting in its infancy now.

Incredibly, it is possible to see something even more extreme than disembodied human minds linked with an avatar. You will be able to detach not just your physical body, but also your actual thoughts. "Mind posting," "whole thoughts emulation," or "mind transfer" is the process of shifting the substance of a scientific thoughts into a PC. There are several suggested techniques by which thoughts posting could be performed. Before you dismiss such concepts as flights of wild imagination, consider this: In October of 2018, scientists have already linked three brains into a network.

"Neuroscientists have successfully hooked up a three-way brain connection to allow three people share their thoughts – and in this case, play a Tetris-style game. The team thinks this wild experiment could be scaled up to connect whole networks of people, and yes, it's as weird as it sounds."[32]

Even with the exponential growth of the technology, applications such as mind posting, or consciousness transference, if it turns out to be feasible at all, will first happen in the 2040's, based on the degree of details that is needed to catch all essential details in the neuronal framework of a natural thoughts. Significant computer handling power and electronic details storage would be needed to digitalize and run a efficient analogue of the brain's ~100 billion connecting nerves. An entire industry of spiritual and philosophical issues such as the lifestyle of a spirit and the characteristics of "self" will have to study and eventually determine if any degree of technical expertise will ever allow a scientific awareness to be moved to synthetic substrate.

Once submitted, thoughts would never die, existing only as pure data and information detached from the human body. The publish would be considered a form of synthetic intellect, sometimes known to as an "infomorph" or "noomorph." An electronic thought could be secured, duplicated, or re-booted at various set points, raising exciting questions regarding personality and identification.

The scenario painted above is one of many hypotheses that will keep the technology of virtual reality going for a long time.

---

[32] https://www.sciencealert.com/brain-to-brain-mind-connection-lets-three-people-share-thoughts

CHAPTER 17
CONTENT IS KING

What does the future of virtual look like from here? This question can be a bit tricky because most people have always looked at the advancement of virtual reality only from the angle of the hardware and software development. But less concern has been given to its contents. This is what might eventually determine if virtual reality will survive the future or not. It should not be assumed that there will be a ready content for the virtual environment.

A combination of great immersive technology with a robust content is what will give inseparable user attachment and eventual fulfilment that users are looking for. The earlier the companies start researching into the unique contents that can actively drive the technology, the better and faster it will meet up with future taste of its potential users.

Asides content quality, virtual reality has two extremely potent and effective attribute that will keep it with us for a very long time. These attributes of virtual reality include its potency to make users escape reality and also relive reality.

- **Escape Reality**: This is already happening. With virtual reality, you can experience unlimited reality; especially in gaming. This is possible in most Role-Playing Games [RPG], where you are in a world of fantasy, disconnected from the busy and noisy real world into a virtual world that you can control and determine. Also, the sense of reward in those games and the dissociation from social statues, economic and emotional reality is a plus.
  An example is the Microtransaction features of Facebook which makes users earn real money and at the same time demystifies the anonymity of the user when entering his details for the transactions.
- **Relive Reality**: Virtual reality isn't just for games. When people can get the opportunity to 'attend' that dream concert,

visit the zoo and touch that animal that would have been untouchable in reality, visit re-invented museums, and be a part of the builders erecting the pyramids of Egypt, then a great feat would have been achieved towards making virtual reality an enduring technology. With this, we can make virtual reality the extension of our real world.

Until another more immersive trend like science fictions writers vision of "teleportation" or similar concepts is made into technology and made real, virtual reality will remain with us for many decades, if not centuries to come.

CHAPTER 18
CONCLUSION

Virtual Reality is reaching the point of acceptance that allows it to be a disruptive force in many markets, and yet is in its earliest stages form a mass audience adoption standpoint. From marketing to job training, medicine to design, virtual reality has been adopted by visionaries, and now is filtering down to the masses. As adoption increases so do the market pressures for innovation and cost reduction. The technologies that deliver our virtual reality experience are growing at exponential rates and so is the quality of the experience they provide to the users. Entire industries are popping up to take advantage of virtual reality, not only in existing markets, but are looking for new and innovative ways to profit from the technology or by providing content.

As we look at what the virtual reality experience will look like in 5, 10, 50 years from now, there are many exciting possibilities. There are also so moral and ethical issues that must be considered as the technology becomes more prevalent. And there is no mistaking that is will continue to become more widely accepted and utilized as we move forward.

I firmly believe that now is the time to look for ways to become part of the tidal wave of disruption that this technology is being to market. You can either ride the wave, or be swept up by it.

www.ingramcontent.com/pod-product-compliance
Lightning Source LLC
Chambersburg PA
CBHW030449220526
45464CB00006B/2460